Understanding MYSELF

by Mary C. Lamia, PhD

A kid's guide to intense emotions and strong feelings

Magination Press
American Psychological Association
Washington, DC

This book is dedicated to all the kids who have told me about their intense emotions and strong feelings—MCL

Published by
MAGINATION PRESS®
An Educational Publishing Foundation Book
American Psychological Association
750 First Street, NE
Washington, DC 20002

For more information about our books, including a complete catalog, please write to us, call 1-800-374-2721, or visit our website at www.apa.org/pubs/magination.

Book and cover design by Naylor Design, Inc., Washington, DC
Printed by Worzalla, Stevens Point, Wisconsin

Library of Congress Cataloging-in-Publication Data
Lamia, Mary C.
  Understanding myself : a kid's guide to intense emotions and strong feelings / by Mary C. Lamia.
      p. cm.
  Includes bibliographical references.
  ISBN-13: 978-1-4338-0889-0 (hbk. : alk. paper)
  ISBN-10: 1-4338-0889-7 (hbk. : alk. paper)
  ISBN-13: 978-1-4338-0890-6 (pbk. : alk. paper)
  ISBN-10: 1-4338-0890-0 (pbk. : alk. paper) 1. Emotions in children—Juvenile literature. 2. Emotions—Juvenile literature. I. Title.

  BF723.E6L35 2011
  155.4'124—dc22

                                                                          2010023483

First Printing September 2010

10 9 8 7 6 5 4

Contents

Getting to Know Yourself

Inside of you is a wealth of information, but it's in another language—the language of emotions. If you could translate it, you'd be able to improve your self-awareness, social relationships, decision-making skills, self-control, and your ability to take action and achieve your goals. In other words, you'd understand yourself better!

You may be surprised to find out where emotions come from and how you experience strong feelings. This book will help you understand what triggers certain emotions, the feelings and thoughts they create, and what you can do when it seems as though they're just too much to handle. With this information you might learn how to accurately and appropriately express yourself, and that will help other people better understand you, too! And, as a bonus, you might learn how to understand the emotions of others.

You'll likely be interested in the *Psych Notes* I've included in the book. These are boxes filled with actual research by psychologists who study emotions. For example, you'll find out if you really can escape from a bad mood, if certain odors affect who or what you like, if bullies really do have low self-esteem, and if smiling can make you happier. These *Psych Notes* will give you a chance to compare your own experiences with what researchers have discovered.

I've included quizzes in the book where you can take a deeper look at yourself. For example, you can ask yourself if you are likely to be envious or jealous, if you are fear seeking, if you are true to your conscience, or if you would put a guy down if he cried. Also, at the end of each part, I've listed some questions for you to ponder that relate back to what I've talked about in the previous chapters.

In my work as a psychologist, young people talk to me about their thoughts, feelings, and experiences. I've shared in this book what kids have told me when they were talking about their intense emotions and strong feelings. You may find that you've felt just like they have. With all this information, I hope you will begin to understand your emotions and how they make you feel.

All my best on your journey to understand yourself!

—*Dr. Mary*

Part one
Feeling
YOUR
Emotions

Imagine ignoring your emotions and what they make you feel.
If you did, you would not be disgusted about eating something
that was rotten, a dangerous situation would not make you frightened,
and you might not react negatively to a friend who always hurts you.
You wouldn't even care if someone likes you or about getting the
award you've won! So one purpose of emotions is to provide you
with information about a situation that can help you to respond
or make decisions.

Your emotions also send information to others through your facial expressions or body language. Your ability to interpret the emotions of others helps you to make sense of what they express and know how to respond to it. But while your emotions convey information to others and to yourself, your emotional response to a situation may differ from that of another person because the same situation can have different meanings for different people. For example, if your friend is terribly afraid of spiders and you aren't afraid of them at all, a huge spider crawling out from under the teacher's desk would create different emotional responses in each of you. She might be afraid and lift up her feet. You might just be amused and smile.

You might describe some of your emotions as positive, and others as negative, because of the ways in which emotions make you feel. But emotions are not necessarily good or bad. Even though we can consider them as positive or negative, you'll find as you read the next chapter that there's much more to experiencing an emotion than whether or not it makes you feel good. In fact, there are many ways in which those so-called negative emotions are just as useful to you as the positive ones.

Chapter 1

The Science Behind Your Emotions

Every day is filled with situations that cause you to respond emotionally. Emotional responses (the feelings and thoughts that are created by your emotions) are signals that allow you to react, protect yourself, communicate, and make decisions. Without having to take the time to think about a situation, your brain instantly creates an action to help you respond.

Your Emotional Brain

Your emotions are in your brain even though you feel them in your body. Your feelings are created by signals sent from your brain that activate the *nervous system* of your body, which affects your muscles and organs. Depending on the emotional response that is signaled by your brain, your nervous system can do things like boost or lower your heart rate, cause your hands to sweat, make your mouth dry, or help you rest. It can even create a feeling of butterflies in your stomach or a lump in your throat.

This is all because your brain has the ability to size up circumstances and automatically create an emotional response that is experienced cognitively (through your thoughts) and physiologically (in your body) as a feeling. Psychologists call it an *appraisal system*. Your brain's appraisal system instantly sizes up a situation and triggers an emotional response even before you are aware you're thinking about it. So if a certain situation causes your brain's appraisal system to trigger the emotion of anger, then you will think negatively and feel irritable. Or if it triggers sadness, then you will think unhappy thoughts and have a heavy feeling in your chest. Your brain will do its best to give you information and help you respond to a situation by having you experience an emotion. However, your appraisal system may not always make the right choice when it triggers an emotion, and I'll tell you more about that later.

The Qualities of an Emotion

Now that you know where emotions come from, can you describe what makes something an emotion? Well, this would lead you right into a scientific controversy. For now, let's go along with a definition of emotion that is often used by psychologists and other emotion researchers:

* *Emotions are automatic and reflexive.* That is, an emotion is a reaction to something and has a particular reason behind it. You may experience disgust *because* you stepped in dog poop and you can smell it on your shoe.

* *Emotions cause body and behavior changes.* The smell of the dog poop on your shoe causes your nervous system to react, and the smell makes you feel sick to your stomach and want to get away from it.

* *Emotional responses give you quick information about a situation that can lead you to take action.* In the situation of your smelly shoe, you might be motivated to leave it outside and be more careful about where you step.

Decisions, Emotions, and Feelings

The idea that your brain automatically makes decisions and triggers an emotion, which then creates a feeling in your body, may sound very strange. But the most important purpose of this process is to give you information about a situation that can help you to decide what to do—an action you should take or a goal you should pursue. Here is an example. Suppose you are walking down the hallway at school, and as you turn the corner you see the person you really like who then smiles at you. You suddenly become very alert and have that excited feeling of butterflies in your stomach.

What does this have to do with your brain? When you saw the person you really like who was smiling at seeing you, your brain instantly— before you knew it—recognized the person, evaluated the situation, and triggered emotions that activated your nervous system which then made you feel alert and excited. But how exactly did your brain help you? Well, it helped you interpret what the person you like was doing—smiling at seeing you—as exciting, which then created the feeling of butterflies in your stomach.

If the other person had behaved as though you didn't exist, your brain would also instantly evaluate the situation and would likely trigger an emotion that would create feelings of discouragement in you. All of this happens in less than a blink of an eye!

Psych Notes !

Facial Expressions Around the World

Researchers have studied facial expressions of people in different cultures and found that particular facial expressions fit with emotions in people from all cultures. Kids all over the world show very similar facial expressions when they experience excitement, surprise, fear, sadness, anger, disgust, embarrassment, and many other emotions. So a kid walking into his surprise birthday party in China might look really astonished, just like kids in France or the United States might. But one of the things that may differ are social rules about expressing emotions. In some cultures, it may be acceptable to cry loudly when you are sad, but in other cultures it may be more appropriate to express your sadness quietly or even hide your feelings. So while certain facial expressions might be shared by all people, there are cultural differences—or learned behaviors—that teach us how to verbally or physically express those emotions, including how intensely we express them.

Ekman, P. (1993). Facial expression and emotion. *American Psychologist, 48,* 384–392.

Paying Attention to Your Emotions

If things don't go your way—for example, when the person you're into doesn't give signs of liking you back—you might want to ignore your emotions. You may not like the information you received through your negative feelings. But ignoring your emotions and not listening to the feelings they create can get in the way of doing something that might lead to a more positive outcome, such as being into someone else. Pay attention. Think about your emotional responses. Figure out what they are telling you.

However, it's also important to consider the way in which your brain interprets situations and whether or not it is accurate. Sometimes your brain might not interpret a situation accurately because of your past experiences. You may have had an experience that led your brain to decide upon the best emotional response based on that one experience. Then you may have that same response to similar situations even if it is not appropriate. For example, maybe you were afraid when a barking dog charged at you. That could have led your brain to appraise all similar situations—seeing any dog on the street—as one where you should become afraid.

You may also want to think about the intensity of your response. Are you conveying the right intensity—too much or too little—of an emotion for a given situation? The intensity and manner in which you respond emotionally communicates what you feel to others. How much you show your emotion and the way in which you show it tells people what you feel. So if a person you like does not smile back at you, then crying and running away might be a reaction that is much too intense (and dramatic) for the situation. On the other hand, you might be sad, but express it in an inappropriate way by saying something mean to the other person.

You now understand that your emotions are signals that are sent from your brain that automatically create a response in your body as feelings. The way in which you express a given emotion, aside from your facial expression, may differ from your friends' depending upon what a particular situation means to you, the intensity in which you express your emotions, and how appropriately you might express yourself. Emotions happen quickly, but what about those times when an emotion seems to hang around for a long time? These are moods, which will be the subject of the next chapter.

Chapter 2

Moods, Emotions, and Feelings

When was the last time you were in a really good mood? What about a really bad one? What is a mood anyway? Before we move on, let's talk about moods and how they relate to feelings and emotions.

Moods and Emotions

Often a mood is not about anyone or anything in particular—it just sits there inside of you. Most psychologists do not consider moods to be "genuine" emotions, but instead as general feelings that stay with you for a while.

However, a mood can influence how you think about or respond to a situation. The feelings created by your mood provide information to your appraisal system—the way your brain automatically sizes up a situation and then responds with a certain emotion. Moods have a particular kind of power because they can influence the judgment and decision-making ability of your appraisal system.

Let's go back to the situation mentioned earlier where you are walking down the hallway at school, and as you turn the corner you see the person you really like who is smiling. But this time, for some unexplained reason, you are in an awful mood that causes you to feel bad about yourself. So when you see the person smiling, you don't think that the smile is because that person is into you. Because your mood makes you not like yourself much, you are not likely to think the other person likes you. Instead you feel uncomfortable and look away. So you can see how your mood might influence your brain's appraisal of the situation.

Moods and Feelings

Moods are powerful and seem to take over your feelings. There are times when you might even realize that you responded in a particular way to a person or situation because of your mood. However, sometimes a mood can be pushed aside by a strong feeling. Going back to suddenly seeing the person you like, it's possible that any excitement you might feel could instantly change your bad mood into a good one. But you don't have to wait for something exciting to come along in order to change your bad mood to a good one! There's a simple way in which you can get yourself out of a bad mood.

Psych Notes !

Escaping From a Bad Mood

When you're in the trenches of a bad mood it may seem as though there is no way out of it. But researchers have found that distraction is a great way to beat a mood. Taking your mind off of your mood-related thoughts can actually change it to neutral. So what should you do with that negative mood? Distract yourself. Spend time in an activity with friends or family, organize your closet, read a good book, or focus on something that grabs your attention—anything, except for how you are feeling.

Erber, R., & Tesser, A. (1992). Task effort and the regulation of mood: The absorption hypothesis. *Journal of Experimental Social Psychology, 28,* 339–359.

In a Mood to Ponder

* Have you ever decided what a friend might be feeling based on his or her facial expression? Were you correct?

* When was the last time you were in a good mood? Did you just happen to wake up that way or did it start because of an experience you had?

* What would you do to change your bad mood to a good one?

Part two

Feeling Self-Conscious

blamed * uncovered * uncomfortable * hesitant

confident * dishonored * confused * exposed

satisfied * ashamed * fulfilled * awkward

humiliated * inhibited * special

There are times when you may be more aware of yourself than usual and think that others are noticing you as well—whether it's when your teacher announces that you've won the essay contest or when you trip and fall on the way to your classroom seat. The emotions of embarrassment, guilt, shame, and pride are generally called the self-conscious emotions because you are very aware of yourself when you experience them. This leads you to you either praise or criticize yourself.

Embarrassment, guilt, or shame may cause you to think that other people are judging you in the same negative way that you may be judging yourself when you feel them. So being caught up in these self-conscious emotions, where you are hyper-aware of yourself in a negative way, can make you want to hide or wish that you could be invisible. But the self-conscious emotion of pride can make you very positively self-aware, creating a great sense of confidence in yourself that you may want to show others. Let's learn more about these emotions.

Chapter 3

Embarrassment

When you are embarrassed, you feel as though everyone sees or knows something about you that you'd like to hide. If a friend or family member reveals something personal about you to others, or if a situation uncovers something about you that you'd prefer to keep private, or if you make a big mistake, then you are likely to experience embarrassment.

Embarrassment signals to others that you don't feel good about something you've done or about something that has happened to you. Since embarrassment makes you claim responsibility for whatever has happened—instantly regretting that you blurted something out—it also makes you assume that others will be critical of you as well.

It's hard enough to be responsible for your own embarrassments, but you may also feel responsible for the embarrassing behavior of your parents, siblings, or friends. People often believe that the behavior of family members or friends will influence their own social

> "Embarrassment is such a big thing at my school. There are so many things that can happen in school to make you feel embarrassed."
> —*Lisa*

Should a Friend's Behavior Embarrass You?

Do people actually judge others by what their friends do? When your friend behaves in a socially inappropriate way, you may believe, as many people do, that your own reputation is going to be affected. Researchers studied six different situations in which observers rated people who were associated with someone whose behavior was publicly offensive—a nose-picker or a loud burper. The people who were associated with the offensive friends most often felt that they would be judged in a negative way, along with the offending person. However, observers did not harshly judge the people who were associated with the offenders. So when a friend makes big social mistake, good news. Other people are busy focusing on your friend and not on you.

Fortune, J. L., & Newby-Clark, I. R. (2008). My friend is embarrassing me: Exploring the guilty by association effect. *Journal of Personality and Social Psychology, 95,* 1440–1449.

standing. This is not true according to research that has been done on the issue. Even so, it might feel true to you. When your parents or siblings interact with your friends, you may certainly feel as though you will be judged by what they say or do.

But what about your parents or your siblings? Lucky for you, just like your loud-burping friend, the behavior of your parents or siblings is what is being noticed, not you! Even so, it might be uncomfortable to deal with. You might become unfairly critical of a sibling or parent or a friend because you are so concerned about what people think of you. In these situations, try to remember that you will not be judged because of another person. Instead, try to be respectful. Being critical will only make you look bad. So when your mom dances like a chicken, remember she's the one who looks like a chicken, not you.

People respond in many different ways to their own embarrassment. A person may express anger, become tearful, want to hide, or just laugh. Many people blush.

Blushing

If you are embarrassed you might blush—your face will feel hot and turn red. Why and how people blush is very technical, but it is so interesting that I will tell you the basics of it. Blushing happens when an emotional trigger causes your glands to release the hormone *adrenalin* in your body. Adrenalin has an effect on your nervous system, which in turn causes the capillaries that carry blood to your skin to widen. Since more blood is able to flow beneath the surface of your skin, it causes you to turn red. Amazing, isn't it?

Controlling a blushing response is very hard, if not impossible, to do. If you blush when you get embarrassed, you may have to deal with everyone noticing your red face. Even worse, they might laugh or point out to others that you are turning red. You will just have to wait a few minutes for your color to change back to normal. Take a deep breath because it will help your body to calm down.

We aren't always in control of whether or not we express strong feelings. Blushing can expose you, especially when you are nervous around someone you like. Your blush signals that you are self-conscious about your feelings. You may not be able to say what you want to say, but your blush is saying something for you.

"I used to turn red when I would say something and felt it was really dumb." *Omar*

"When I am around boys that I like, I get nervous and blush. I wonder what they are going to do or if they like me or not." *Haley*

Psych Notes !

How Blushing May Help You

People who blush often wish they could hide that emotional expression from others. But what do other people think about the person who blushes? A study investigated how people evaluated someone who blushed and someone who did not blush from a mistake or mishap. They found that, in most instances, those who blushed were evaluated more favorably in terms of trustworthiness or sympathy than those who did not. The investigators concluded that blushing can positively help the way in which others judge you. So go ahead and blush! Blushing can help your reputation and won't hurt it.

Dijk, C., de Jong, P. J., & Peters, M. L. (2009). The remedial value of blushing in the context of transgressions and mishaps. *Emotion, 9,* 287–291.

Embarrassing Mistakes

Have you ever been embarrassed about making a mistake? Everybody makes mistakes and most people wish they could undo what they did and take it back.

Have you ever made a mistake and then you think about it over and over again? Thinking about it just makes you even more aware of yourself and how awful it feels to have made the mistake. This can feel like a punishment. So here are some ideas for getting over an embarrassing mistake:

* *Laugh at yourself!* Everyone will laugh with you and then it will be over. Remember that thinking about an embarrassment is not going to change the past. You can punish yourself all day and it's not going to change a thing.

How Much Does Stuff Embarrass You?

Rate yourself on each of the following statements using a scale from 1 (do not agree) to 5 (strongly agree):

_____ I don't like it when friends talk about something cool I'm wearing.

_____ I like playing games, but it's embarrassing to lose.

_____ I feel awful when I have to read out loud in class.

_____ I get embarrassed about what family members say or do around my friends.

_____ When I don't feel good about how I look, I don't want anyone to see me.

_____ It wouldn't be fun if my friends teased me about the person I like.

_____ Total

What about your score?

20–30: You are probably pretty sensitive to embarrassment. Just remember that it's normal to get embarrassed about stuff at your age.

6–20: Not a lot of blushing for you! You are not likely to get embarrassed by many situations, and you probably don't take it too personally if an embarrassing situation happens.

* Forgive yourself and move on. Remind yourself that you're human.
* Remember that most people are unlikely to care about what happened as much as you will. (Really, do you think about other people's mistakes all the time? Not likely.)
* Don't take it seriously when any one laughs at you, as though your reputation is ruined forever. There will always those people who

will remind you about the silly stuff you've done because they don't want to think about their own mistakes.

When you make a mistake —trip and fall in front of the entire school, blurt out that you like a guy or girl—brush it off and forget about it because it is most likely that others will not judge you for doing something silly or embarrassing. Do whatever you can to correct yourself for that next time. You can change your behavior in the future if you can learn from the past.

Being embarrassed or avoiding embarrassment may be a big deal in your life. But now that you know a little more about this intense emotion —how you respond to embarrassment and how others respond to you in embarrassing situations—you might be able to deal with it better when you get embarrassed. And you know that will happen!

Do you think it is easier to forget about an embarrassment than it is to let go of something that makes you feel guilty? Maybe it will be easier to answer that question after reading the next chapter about guilt, another self-conscious emotion.

"Being embarrassed is the hardest feeling for me to feel. Like sometimes if you fart in class—it happened to me. Everyone around me laughed, but I felt totally embarrassed."
Jason

Chapter 4

Guilt

When you believe that your actions have hurt someone in a physical, emotional, or moral way, you are likely to experience guilt. Guilt makes you blame yourself and it can make you feel like you have a knot in your stomach or a lump in your throat. Guilt preoccupies your thoughts, so you might think about that situation over and over, worry about what others will think of you, or just not like yourself.

When you were very young, you learned about ideas, such as what is right or wrong, what is good or bad—things that are often considered by many people as appropriate ways to act. These are called social standards. Doing the right thing or being good is also connected with being loved and getting approval from parents, caregivers, teachers, friends, and others, and overall, feeling like you are a good person. You've taken on the social standards of your parents and the people who are important to you, and formed your own conscience— a sense of right and wrong.

Guilt has a lot to do with your conscience. Your conscience is like a little judge in your head that evaluates your behavior and decides if you have lived up to those expected social standards. When you're faced with making decisions about what you should or shouldn't do, you usually rely on your conscience. If you go against your standards, then you might be betraying yourself and not listening to your own conscience. And then you might feel guilty. So if you value honesty and think that lying is not a behavior that is acceptable to you, then you might feel guilty if you lie. Think about the last time you felt guilty. Why did you feel that way?

Guilt Serves A Purpose

Your standards offer guidelines that help you decide if what you think and do is acceptable. Not everyone has the same standards that you do. Some people are very careful about doing what they believe is the right thing. In fact, there are people who might be too careful about doing the right thing all of the time because they experience intense guilt if they don't. Becoming preoccupied with doing the right thing (like being good all the time) can be just as hard on you as neglecting your standards.

But you may have noticed that there are people who do not seem to experience guilt or can disregard their guilt when they harm others. Imagine how hard it would be if all the kids at your school (except you) didn't have the emotion of guilt that makes them be true to their standards. You might find many kids lying, cheating, stealing, or hurting others (if they otherwise didn't care about getting into trouble). So guilt serves a good purpose in social relationships because it

What Do You Feel Guilty About?

Researchers studied fifth, eighth, and eleventh graders to find out if boys and girls were different in terms of what makes them feel guilty. Girls were more likely than boys to mention feeling guilty about social situations where they lied, broke a trust, or were inconsiderate to others. More boy students compared with girl students mentioned guilt about behaviors such as fighting or damaging property that belongs to others. Neither girls nor boys were more likely to feel more guilt about their inner thoughts or about breaking rules—like skipping school, being disobedient, or stealing. If you asked all the kids in your class what makes them feel guilty, do you think you'd get similar results?

Williams, C., & Bybee, J. (1994). What do children feel guilty about? Developmental and gender differences. *Developmental Psychology, 30*, 617–623.

can help people get along. Remembering that people's standards might differ from yours can help you better understand situations where you are not treated in the way in which you treat others.

Guilt Can Protect You

If your guilt can keep you from hurting yourself or others, then the emotion of guilt protects you, doesn't it? Well, if your brain is properly evaluating the situation based on similar past experiences, then the answer is yes. For example, what if you really want to fit in with friends who do things that go against your standards—things that

Are You True to Your Conscience?

Check *true* or *false* in answer to the following statements:

TRUE   **FALSE**

____   ____   I sometimes lie when I'm asked if I finished doing something I was supposed to do when really I haven't done it.

____   ____   If I am afraid of getting into trouble. I may not always tell the truth.

____   ____   My friends don't really expect me to apologize if I hurt their feelings.

____   ____   Sometimes when I do something wrong, I just wait and hope that no one will notice.

____   ____   Most people will just forget about what you do that hurts them, so you might as well forget about it yourself.

____   ____   If you just don't admit that you did something wrong, most of the time you can get away with it.

____   ____   TOTAL

What about your score?
If you answered three or more of the questions as *true*, you may think that it is easier to ignore your conscience and avoid your feelings of guilt. If friends and family members know that you are truthful, and that you are first to admit when you are wrong or have done something wrong, then they will always trust your words. If you answered four or more of the questions as *false,* then it's likely that listening to your conscience is important to you.

might even hurt you? Fortunately, good old guilt happens to come along when you do something that goes against what you expect of yourself. And if you do something, even though doing it makes you feel guilty, you may also have to lie to yourself and justify your behavior by making all sorts of lame excuses. But now that you understand yourself a little better, you know that if you are involved in a situation that goes against your standards, your guilt will try to tell you so. Pay attention to your emotion, honestly decide whether your brain has properly appraised the situation, and be true to yourself.

Guilt is a complicated self-conscious emotion. The good news about guilt is that it can help guide you because it is like an alarm going off that tells you that you've betrayed your own conscience. Emotion researchers generally believe that guilt serves the purpose of helping people get along in their social relationships.

If you have difficulty acknowledging your guilt to yourself, or to someone you've hurt by your actions, it might be because admitting that you are guilty makes you feel ashamed. In this way, guilt and shame are related. So let's move on to the self-conscious emotion of shame.

Chapter 5

Shame

Shame, like guilt, has to do with how you think about yourself. But there is a big difference between guilt and shame. Guilt is tied to doing something that goes against your *social standards,* while shame results from not living up to your ideals—your *personal standards.* You may experience guilt if your actions have hurt others. But shame makes you feel as though your whole self is bad.

Let's say you lied to a friend. You are likely to feel guilty, right? And what if afterward, you begin to feel really bad about lying and decide that a good friend would tell the truth. So, you want to tell your friend that you lied. But what happens if before you can admit your lie, your friend finds out and calls you out on it? You would probably feel ashamed of yourself. You might feel that you have disappointed your friend as well as let yourself down in a big way—that you have not lived up to your own personal standard of being a good friend.

When you feel shame, you can feel disgraced, dishonored, inadequate, undesirable, or flawed. Shame makes you want to hide yourself or just disappear.

Your Ideals and Shame

You might feel shame regarding certain things about yourself if you believe that they don't match up with what you think are good or ideal qualities. This might involve how you look, who your friends are, what you say, or how well you do in school. But if you always compare who you think you are to who you think you should be, then you may never really live up to your own standards.

"Sometimes I think that all my friends are attractive but I'm not. I wish I was taller and that my hair wasn't curly." *Adriana*

Shame That Belongs to Others

Some kids are ashamed of themselves because of situations or circumstances that are beyond their control. Certain circumstances like where you live or characteristics of your family members can be unnecessary sources of shame. Kids can experience shame because they are related to someone who is behaving shamefully or because they believe that their family is not good enough or is "less than" other families in some way. Sometimes when kids are abandoned or if they are emotionally or physically abused by a parent, they take on the shame that belongs to the parent who left or hurt them by assuming that it's because they themselves are the "bad" one.

"I don't like when my friends come to my house because my father acts weird if he's been drinking." *Kalib*

How Do You Measure Up?

Rate yourself on each of the following statements using a scale from 1 (do not agree) to 5 (strongly agree):

_____ I always want to look like someone else.

_____ I feel uncomfortable in my own body and obsess about being either too fat or too thin.

_____ When I don't get a very high grade on a test, I am really hard on myself.

_____ I usually hide my mistakes.

_____ If others really knew how I am inside, they probably wouldn't like me.

What about your score?

20–25: It's time to get a reality check on your ultra high standards. Being this hard on yourself can make you feel miserable. Talk to your parents, a teacher, or a counselor about the way in which you evaluate yourself.

16–20: Take a look at who you are and who you want to be. Then consider whether or not your standards are realistic and achievable, or if you should alter them.

Less than 15: You standards are hopefully realistic and appropriate, and you're not too hard on yourself.

It's hard, but try not to be ashamed because of your circumstances or the behavior of a relative. You must remind yourself that you are a separate person and can't control others or your circumstances.

Shame and Bullying

Shame can feel so awful that some kids try to make themselves feel better by making other kids feel as awful as they do. These are kids who act like a bully toward others. Whether you are a person who bullies others or someone who is the target of someone acting like a bully, it is important to understand how shame plays a part in what happens. People who act like bullies often feel shame about themselves so they may try to "give away" their own shame to someone by making another person feel awful. Kids who bully and tease can figure out what makes other kids feel insecure and use that against them. So bullies avoid dealing with their own insecurities by making others feel insecure or afraid.

"At the talent show two boys were making fun of me because I play the violin. They said I was lame. I wanted to cry, but then they would make fun of me even more." *Mindy*

What You Can Do About Your Shame

Because shame makes you feels undesirable, inferior, or causes you to think that something about yourself is really flawed, what can you do about it? First, as with all of your emotions, it's important to evaluate what triggers shame in you and decide if your brain is appraising the situation correctly.

* Try to keep yourself from getting pushed into feeling shame that really does not belong to you.

Psych Notes !

Do Bullies Have Low Self-Esteem?

People commonly believe that kids who behave like bullies (aggressive and mean) do so because they have low self-esteem. However, many research studies have proven that there is no link between kids who behave aggressively toward other kids and low self-esteem. In fact, psychologists have found that kids who behave like bullies have high self-esteem, but that they are very "shame-prone." That means they are afraid their failures or shortcomings will be exposed. A person can have problems with shame and still have high self-esteem, and this is what makes a person act like a bully. Their mean behavior toward others keeps their self-esteem high because it takes their own and others' attention away from the parts of themselves about which they are ashamed. So when someone acts like a bully around you, you can bet that they have high self-esteem, but they are hiding their shame.

Thomaes, S., Bushman, B. J., Stegge, H., & Olthof, T. (2008). Trumping shame by blasts of noise: Narcissism, self-esteem, shame, and aggression in young adolescents. *Child Development, 79,* 1792–1801.

* Find your confidence. Something that triggers shame in you can make you feel inadequate about your whole self. Separate out what is making you ashamed from everything else about yourself.
* Stand tall and look confident even if you don't feel so sure of yourself inside.
* If you tend to take your shame out on others (like bullying), remind yourself that you want people to respect you rather than be afraid of you.

* Experiment with showing kindness to people and see if that helps you to feel better about yourself.
* Don't be afraid of your weaknesses. They're part of being human.

The emotion of shame can be very painful, and it involves the evaluation of your whole self. Understanding this intense emotion may help you decide if the shame you feel actually has to do with yourself, or if it is the result of your relationship with others, your circumstances, or a specific situation.

Thus far we have taken a look at three self-conscious emotions: embarrassment, guilt, and shame. A fourth self-conscious emotion is pride, which is the subject of the next chapter.

Chapter 6

Pride

Pride is another self-conscious emotion that can make you very aware of yourself. Like embarrassment, guilt, and shame, pride is triggered when you evaluate yourself against some standard. But the difference is that pride can create a great feeling of respect and belief in yourself that makes you want to stand tall.

Accomplishments, achievements, or having qualities or things that are admired by others can make you proud and can give you feelings of great satisfaction. So pride can make you very aware of yourself in a positive way.

A situation where you feel pride can positively affect your self-esteem—the general sense of how you feel about yourself, including your beliefs about your own importance. A circumstance that creates pride and boosts your self-esteem can make you want to work harder in order to keep up that great feeling it gives you.

Reactions to Your Pride

When you are feeling proud, others may be aware of your accomplishment, your personal qualities, or what you have. In social situations, your pride could make you feel either confidently or uncomfortably aware of yourself. Think about the last time you bought cool new clothes. Did you imagine yourself feeling good about wearing them to school? But when you actually wore them to school, and when others kids complimented you, you may have felt very confident or your good feeling may have turned into discomfort.

If others make you feel uncomfortable about things that make you proud, try to step back and realize that their reaction may have more to do with discomfort about themselves (like envy, for example).

Can You Have Too Much Pride?

It's important to have confidence in who you are and to think well of yourself. But it is possible to overvalue yourself. If you value yourself too highly, or appear to be a bit *too* proud of yourself, others might think that you are self-centered. So you want to appear confident, but at the same time be realistic when it comes to evaluating yourself—don't tear yourself down or fill yourself up with fake pride.

People who have a self-important attitude can fool others especially those who leave others out or put down peers. In fact, they may even be seen as popular. So someone who has false pride—an attitude of

"I loved working on my science fair project at school. But when I won an award, my friends just give me a strange look. It made it hard to feel proud of myself."
Katie

"I feel really lucky to have friends who compliment me when I do something well. They help me feel proud of myself and I help them feel that way, too."
Celeste

Popularity and Pride

Verbally or nonverbally, we send emotional messages to others who interpret them. If a person appears really confident, he is expressing pride to others whether or not he intends to do so. Researchers wondered if nonverbal expressions of pride helped people become more popular. They found that people who look proud are thought of by others to have high status, that is, popular and well-liked. If a person's social status is automatically communicated to others, what can you do to make yours look good? Stand tall, appear confident, and work hard to be your best so that you can feel it and show it.

Shariff, A. F., & Tracy, J. L. (2009). Knowing who's boss: Implicit perceptions of status from the nonverbal expression of pride. *Emotion, 9,* 631–639.

superiority that excludes, devalues, or controls others—can become the focus of peers who want that person's approval. If a lot of other people want you to like them because they see you as being "exclusive," then you will seem popular, even if it is popularity that has not been well-earned.

Can You Have Too Little Pride?

It's also possible to undervalue yourself. Your self-esteem might not be so great. You might not see a lot to be proud of in yourself. But it's there! The fact is, being confident will attract people to you. When you are confident and believe in yourself, others usually see you that way

What Triggers Your Pride?

Rate yourself on each of the following statements by checking *true* or *false*:

TRUE   **FALSE**

_____ _____ I have a least one talent that most others don't have.

_____ _____ I can let others know when I've done something well.

_____ _____ I feel good about the work that I turn in at school.

_____ _____ Most of the time I try to do my best, whatever the activity happens to be.

_____ _____ I am a great friend to others.

_____ _____ My family members can always count on me.

What about your score?

If you answered *true* to four or more of the statements, you should be proud of yourself! There are many aspects of your life that are sources of pride for you.

If you answered *true* to three or less of the statements, you may want to take a look at what you can do differently to have more sources of pride in your life.

as well. You don't have to hide all of your insecurities with a fake attitude in order to be confident. Take a look at yourself and be proud of your strengths, talents, and abilities. You don't have to *be* the best at anything in order to have pride in yourself. You simply have to *do* your best.

You've now learned about four self-conscious emotions: embarrassment, guilt, shame, and pride. The next time that you are extremely aware of yourself and don't want anyone else to notice, remember that your self-conscious emotion is making you feel exposed, causing you to you worry about what others think about you, or possibly making you become a bit hard on yourself. Hopefully of all the self-conscious emotions you will experience, the one you'll encounter most will be pride and the self-respect that it can make you feel.

In a Mood to Ponder

* Think about a situation in which you felt embarrassed. What did you do in response to your embarrassment?
* Remember the last time you did something that made you experience guilt. Was it difficult to talk about?
* What would be your response to a friend who felt ashamed of where she lives?
* When a peer experiences pride in an accomplishment, what is your reaction?

Part three

Feeling Threatened

afraid * worried * hesitant * freaked out

tense * nervous * stressed * frightened

terrified * scared * panicked * apprehensive

uneasy * repulsed * upset

Imagine that you are about to give a speech in front of the whole school or that you are in a foreign country and become separated from your family. Threatening situations or circumstances will trigger emotions of anxiety or fear. These emotions can make you feel terribly uncomfortable and unsafe. After all, your brain is telling you so by putting you on high alert—your heart rate will increase, you might sweat, your muscles seem to tighten-up, and you might feel as though you have knots in your stomach. In some situations you might have enormous amounts of energy. In others you might experience a very uncomfortable sensation of doom.

Another emotion that can be triggered by something that is threatening is disgust. But disgust is threatening in a way that is different from anxiety and fear. Disgust makes you repulsed by something or someone. In most situations, disgust actually lowers your heart rate rather than increases it as with anxiety and fear.

In the next chapters, we will take a look at the emotions of anxiety, fear, and disgust and how to deal with them when you feel threatened.

Chapter 7

Anxiety

Do you ever feel jittery, nervous, or a little bit sick to your stomach when you have to give a presentation in class or if you're trying out for a team? You might have anxiety in situations like these where you expect a bad or negative outcome, even if there is no good reason to think so.

When you are anxious, you can feel it in your body as dizziness, restlessness, or as a fidgety feeling. Sweating, blushing, shaking, and feeling downright sick to your stomach can be caused by anxiety, as well as having nightmares or trouble falling asleep. If you are anxious, you may bite your nails, you may want to eat too much, or you might lose your appetite. When you feel anxious, things that may seem easy for others to do may seem difficult for you. But actually, people who have anxiety may not realize that others also might be anxious in certain situations, too. The difference is that some people push themselves past their anxiety while others will avoid the situation.

Feeling Your (Normal) Anxiety

Social, performance, or unfamiliar situations can trigger anxiety and strong feelings of uneasiness or dread. Anxiety isn't always a bad thing, especially when it is a kind of nervous energy that motivates you. But sometimes anxiety can make you worry that you will forget what you have to say. You might also believe that others will judge you negatively. Some people describe situations where they just go "blank" because of their anxiety.

If you've ever frozen from anxiety, know that you're definitely not alone. There are some strategies you can use that might help you overcome an anxious brain that goes blank. Here are a few:

* Give yourself a pep talk that everything is going to turn out fine.
* Practice and prepare as well as you possibly can for what you are going to do.
* Visualize a happy, relaxing, or peaceful place. Use that image to relax your brain in the minute or so before you do what makes you anxious.
* Take a few deep breaths. When people are anxious, they often forget to breathe.
* Move around beforehand. Get some exercise to get rid of your anxious energy.
* Keep doing what makes you anxious. The more you do the things that make you anxious, the less anxious you will be the next time.

Anxiety and Your Social Life

Are you afraid to eat in public, use a school restroom, be away from a parent, or make eye contact with others? Do your feelings get in the way of making friends and being comfortable around other kids? If you answered yes to any of these, you may need some extra help in dealing with your anxiety. Most people who are anxious know that their fears may be unreasonable, but they can't seem to do anything about it.

If you experience intense anxiety in social situations, it's likely that you'll believe it will always happen, so you may avoid them. Living your life avoiding social situations and the anxiety they create could make you more comfortable, but it likely will not help you be fulfilled. You may have to step out of your comfort zone in order to get past your anxiety. Having someone with you to give you support and encouragement will help you during those times when you want to move forward.

But when you are anxious, you may not be able to respond well to people or situations. You may even end up disappointed in yourself or worried about the response of others. If you really like someone, your anxiety can be a pain. You might feel shy and unable to get words out correctly. Your mind might go blank and your mouth might become dry.

When you feel intense anxiety starting to take over in social situations, here are some things you can do:

* *Pay closer attention to the responses of others.* Remember that others might appear shy or withdrawn when they are anxious, too.

> **"I really get nervous in front of the girl I like. I'm always afraid that I won't have anything to say."**
> *Alejandro*

* *Challenge yourself gradually.* If you want to try to do something that usually creates anxiety in you (like making eye contact with others), remember that you don't have to change all at once. Do at least one thing every day that goes beyond your comfort zone.
* *Laugh.* Think of something funny and try to share it with someone else, even if it has to do with the situation and how it makes you anxious. Laughter relieves anxiety because it takes away some of the tension you feel.

Anxiety and Worry

Anxiety is often expressed through worries that are focused on expecting something bad might happen. Worried thoughts make you feel as though you have a knot in your stomach or a lump in your throat or you might feel like you're about to cry.

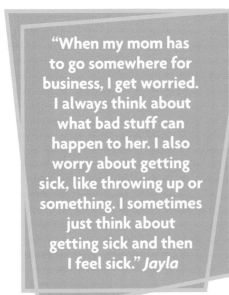

"When my mom has to go somewhere for business, I get worried. I always think about what bad stuff can happen to her. I also worry about getting sick, like throwing up or something. I sometimes just think about getting sick and then I feel sick." *Jayla*

When you worry, it may seem as though you are also trying to prepare yourself for something that you think is going to happen. Worry involves wanting to control something or wanting to make a situation different. That's why when you are worried you can't get something out of your mind. You think about the worry over and over again as though you will find a solution if you think about it enough.

You might worry about a lot of different things—your grades, fitting in, how you look, problems in the world, or your future. If you hear your parents fighting you might worry that they will get divorced. A big worry for young people is that something bad might happen to their parents. This worry seems reasonable because parents are there to protect you, and you would feel vulnerable without them.

Anxiety and Stress

Lots of people use the word "stress" when they really mean anxiety. But experiences that cause a lot of anxiety in your life can then create a stress response. In other words, stress is a reaction triggered by outside forces. Stress reactions include physical changes in your body such as a rapid heartbeat, sweating, dry mouth, or shortness of breath. And they can cause behavior changes like being grumpy or worried. It's normal to have some stress in your life. You may be stressed at a particular time because you have so much to do. However, the stress itself can cause you to have difficulty concentrating and getting started on things, or it can make you feel totally disorganized.

What You Can Do About Your Anxiety, Worry, or Stress

Anxiety, worry, or stress can be really overwhelming. Here are some things you can do about it:

* Talk about your anxiety, worries, or stress with your parents or with someone you trust.
* Take a warm bath or a shower.
* Exercise or take a fast walk every day.
* Listen to music and dance.
* Do something that calms you. Take deep breaths, close your eyes, and try to clear your mind.

"My friend is always stressed. It's really hard for me to see him like that. If anyone says one word to him he can cry or get upset. I want to comfort him, but it seems like I can't. Sometimes he gets really mad and screams into his sweatshirt. He gets all out of whack." *Donovan*

Psych Notes !

Getting Past Stress

Some people are thought to be more "resilient" than others. That means when they experience a negative situation, they seem to bounce back more quickly than people generally do. What makes these people different? According to researchers, people who recover most effectively from stressful times have learned to recognize the effects of stressful situations, and they are able to think about positive outcomes by using positive emotions. You can create a positive emotion through the use of humor, optimistic thinking, or relaxation techniques.

Tugade, M. M., & Frederickson, B. L. (2004). Resilient individuals use positive emotions to bounce back from negative emotional experiences. *Journal of Personality and Social Psychology, 86,* 320–333.

* Make sure you get enough sleep every night.
* Keep your life and your room organized. Create a schedule for getting things done. Make a list of all that you want or need to do so you won't forget anything.

Motivational Styles and Anxiety

People have different ways in which they complete tasks, including how they manage time. If your teacher assigns a project that is due in two weeks, some of your classmates, the do-it-ahead-of-time people, might feel anxious and pressured until they get the project finished. Yet another group of students will postpone doing the assignment and they may even delay starting to do it until the deadline is very close. These people are often called *procrastinators.* However, that term has come to have a negative meaning. There is no right or

What Is Your Motivational Style?

Check *true* or *false* in answer to the following questions:

TRUE	FALSE	
_____	_____	If I have time I like to start projects when they are assigned.
_____	_____	I seem to have a better time hanging out with friends if I know the things that I am supposed to do that day are done.
_____	_____	When I finish an assignment early, I don't look at it again or check it.
_____	_____	It is hard for me to ignore things until the last minute if they need to get done.
_____	_____	If I have too much to do, I am stressed until everything is finished.
_____	_____	My homework is almost never the last thing I do before going to bed.
_____	_____	TOTAL

What about your score?

If you answered three or more of the questions as *true*, you likely have a do-it-ahead style. (Be sure to check your work before you turn it in.) If you answered *true* to two questions or less, you may be more motivated to finish tasks when you are close to a deadline. Always check-in with yourself afterward about whether or not you gave yourself enough time to complete the task with your best work. If you needed a bit more time, remember to give that to yourself for your next big assignment.

wrong motivational style—a person can be very effective or very ineffective using either style.

People who postpone doing things seem to need the anxiety and pressure caused by a close deadline in order to motivate themselves to get things done. Other people don't like to wait. In fact, they need to get things done early because they have anxiety and pressure until tasks are completed.

What counts for each style is that the completion of the task reflects your best work. Doing something ahead of time can result in hurried and messy work just as it can by doing it at the last minute. Whatever your motivational style, just make certain that it lets you do your best, and that it shows.

Normal anxiety can express itself in social or performance situations, through worrying, and even in your particular motivational style. Most anxiety is going to pass, along with the situation or circumstance that created it.

Another emotion that often feels threatening is fear, which will be discussed in the next chapter. You'll find that some human responses to fear are similar to those that are felt with anxiety.

Chapter 8

Fear

Everyone feels afraid sometimes. If you didn't have the emotion of fear, you wouldn't be able to protect yourself and respond well to dangerous or threatening situations. People have *automatic fears* (ones that you were born with) and *learned fears* (ones that you have acquired). Automatic fears can be things that startle you (like someone suddenly throwing a ball at you), loud noises, and being separated from parents. But most fears, like being afraid of flying or insects, are learned.

People become frightened when they feel unsafe or when they are in danger. Not everything that triggers a fear response is actually dangerous, but it still may feel that way. And fear can be triggered from past experiences when a similar situation reminds you of something frightening that happened before (like being afraid of wasps because you were stung by one).

Fear is experienced very much like anxiety. The difference is that fear is a response to actual danger or from a memory of something threatening. Anxiety is a more general expectation that something bad is going to happen. So you might be anxious because you're going on a trip and wonder if there are any wasps at that place. And you might experience fear if you get there and actually see a wasp buzzing around you.

How Your Body Responds to Fear

When you are afraid your feelings are like warning signs from your brain telling you that you are in danger, even if the danger is imagined. Your brain automatically prepares your body in a way that will make you better able to respond to your fear. This is commonly called a "fight-or-flight response." Your heart rate will increase and your blood pressure and body temperature will rise. A frightening movie can create a similar response, even though you are safe on your couch at home. But your brain's appraisal system doesn't necessarily know the difference. It just wants you to take action to protect yourself.

"I am afraid of the dark. It's because of not knowing what's around me when it's really dark. I get up to get a drink of water and my floor makes a sound and it's freaky like somebody is there." *Sophie*

Nighttime Fears

Your thoughts can stir up a fear response. Have you ever had one of those creepy feelings, the kind where you're in bed at night and hear a noise, so you wonder if something or someone is out there, or worse yet, you imagine that someone or something is in your house? Your imagination can come up with amazing possibilities when everything is quiet. Sometimes people have frightening thoughts and feelings after reading a book, seeing a movie, or after being told something scary. Other times those creepy, scary thoughts seem to come from nowhere.

Psych Notes !

Fight, Flight, or Do Something Else?

The term "fight-or-flight response" describes the behavior of various animals when they are threatened. Animals either hang around and fight or take off in order to escape danger. Yet scientists have recognized that animals and people have other responses to a threat. For example, a person or animal might stand still, play dead, or just "freeze" in response to being threatened. You might yell and scream as a fighting response rather than get physical. Or your flight response could be going to your room to be alone. So some researchers have suggested an expanded version of the fight-or-flight response called "freeze, flight, fight, or fright." Other scientists have suggested that "tend-and-befriend" responses should also be considered. These include behaviors such as turning to others for help or social support or making a situation less tense, dangerous, or uncomfortable in some way. However we consider them, responses to threat are automatic and fascinating.

Bracha, H., Ralston, T. C., Matsukawa, J. M., Matsunaga, S., Williams, A. E., & Bracha, A. S. (2004). Does "fight or flight" need updating? *Psychosomatics, 45,* 448–449; and Taylor, S. E., Klein, L. C., Lewis, B. P., Gruenewald, T. L., Gurung, R. A., & Updegraff, J. A. (2000). Biobehavioral responses to stress in females: Tend-and-befriend, not fight-or-flight. *Psychological Review, 107,* 411–429.

Scary Dreams

As you sleep, your mind can be very creative and can make up incredible dreams that are like movies in your head. When dreams are scary you become frightened exactly the way you do when things in real life make you scared. Your brain sends signals to your body to respond as though the situation is real. Thoughts and emotions that are floating around inside your head—including those that make you anxious, afraid, or upset—can become a scary dream. Scary dreams could be about anything.

Dreams serve many purposes. They are a way to work out feelings that you have had during the day. Sometimes scary dreams are also a way for you to remind yourself that feeling protected, prepared, and safe are very important.

When you have a scary dream, don't let that fear take over! Here are some things to do to comfort yourself:

* Give your scary dream a good ending when you wake up. Think about the dream and create a situation in your mind about what could happen next that would make you feel safe.
* Tell your dream to someone you trust.
* Write your dream down and make it into a story or a play. Or make it into a drawing or painting. Use it as inspiration.
* Remind yourself that a scary dream won't hurt you. Having a dream does not mean that it will happen.
* Always reassure yourself that everything really is okay.

Fear From Scary Programs, Movies, and News

Have you ever been frightened by a movie, a television program, or something you saw on the news? When people view scary movies or programs, they can become overstimulated. This means that the frightening images or sounds can stick in your mind and keep you stirred up inside. You remember little bits of the scary movie or program when you go to bed or even the next day. It is hard to forget about it. Scary programs or movies can cause you to have nightmares or problems with concentration and attention.

If something you see is violent or scary, it can stay with you in your mind for days. Images are left over and can get in the way of your concentration and attention. So if you have nightmares from watching frightening programs, you are having a reaction because your brain is processing the images as though they are real. If this happens to you, you might decide that watching scary or violent programs is not good for you. You can simply say that you're not going to watch something scary because you don't like the way it makes you feel.

> **"If I watch a scary movie, I see it in my mind and I see it in my dreams. When I have it in my head, I try to think of something else like something fun."**
> *Simon*

Seeking Frightening Situations

Some people practically invite their brain to produce a fear response. They seek out situations that are a little scary, like scary movies or even some risky situations, because it is exciting for them. But it is very important to be safe and know when taking a risk would not be good for you.

Some people seem to have fun scaring their friends by doing something that is startling (like jumping out from behind a bush and screaming just as your unsuspecting friend is walking by). This is usually a way people enjoy sharing an intense emotional experience, similar to the enjoyment some people have when they watch a scary movie together. It's interesting that humans have found ways to use intense fear responses for entertainment. But remember, if your friends don't think that it's fun, don't scare them. And it's just fine to tell others that you don't like being scared if it's not fun for you, either.

Are You Fear-Seeking?

Rate yourself on each of the following statements using a scale from
1 (do not agree) to 5 (strongly agree):

_____ I like it when friends try to scare me with sudden movements or
noises.

_____ Really scary movies are fun to watch.

_____ I think it would be exciting to stay in a house where bats flew in
at night.

_____Things that happen naturally (like lightening, earthquakes, or
tornados) don't bother me.

_____ I usually laugh when everything is safe after a scary situation
(like airplane turbulence).

_____ I always go for the scariest rides at an amusement park.

_____ Total

What about your score?

20–30: You like being scared—safely, of course. You are likely a person
who likes using your fear response for fun.

6–20:   You're probably a bit more cautious about being scared. You are
not likely to seek out frightening situations and you prefer not to
have fear responses just for fun.

What to Do When You Are Afraid

There are a lot of ways to deal with your fears, whether they're in response to a real danger, a past experience, a scary dream, or something like a news show.

* Talk about your fears with someone you trust. Parents, siblings, or friends can help you decide what to do about your fears and can lead you to discover what you can do to make yourself feel safe.
* Ask for reassurance and ask questions. For example, you can ask your parents to check that the doors are locked or you can ask questions about a situation that makes you afraid.
* Get some information. Sometimes knowing the reality of a situation can make it a lot less scary. If you're afraid of flying, learn about what keeps an aircraft up in the air and what creates turbulence.
* Be sure to remind yourself that you have a very creative imagination and things may not be as they seem. Although your fear is not based in reality you may still have a difficult time letting it go. Use that creative imagination to picture yourself in the situation you fear and create a good outcome to the story in your mind.

> "I think kids like to be scared, so they go to scary movies. I think they like the challenge or wonder, what level should I go to next? When I was younger, I went to a scary movie because I just liked the fact that something could scare me. Then I wondered what else I could see that could challenge me. I just wanted to see how scared I could get." *Ryan*

The emotions of anxiety and fear can create an intense response. Anxiety can be experienced in many ways including through worries and even in the kind of motivational style you have. Fear is a response to a threat or danger that causes you to be alert and take action in order to protect yourself. Another emotion that is a response to something threatening is disgust, which is the subject of the next chapter.

Chapter 9

Disgust

Disgust is such an intense emotion that even reading about it in this chapter might trigger the facial expression it creates—your nose twists up, your mouth turns down, and your eyes might squint. It's hard to keep a straight face when you are disgusted! Disgust causes you to experience something as distasteful, revolting, or repulsive. As a result, you might feel sick to your stomach or even gag and feel as though you are going to throw up. Whatever disgusts you might be so disagreeable that you will want to stay away or at least protect your senses so that you won't taste, smell, or see it. But although your disgust might feel awful, this emotional response is one that protects you by making you want to distance yourself from something that is offensive to you.

What's Good About Disgust

Imagine this. You happen to want a glass of milk, but you're not sure if the milk in the refrigerator is still good to drink. So first you smell it. It smells spoiled, so your stomach churns and you gag! You experience disgust. Disgust, like other emotions, helps you make a decision. Your immediate reaction helps you to decide not to drink the milk. In this sense, disgust protects you from drinking or eating anything that might be spoiled or contaminated, which is likely why this emotion is a part of us.

The emotion of disgust might help you to understand your brain's appraisal system—the part that sizes up a situation and triggers an emotional response. For example, if you keep remembering the smell of that spoiled milk, your brain might decide that it should keep you away from all milk. So later on the thought of drinking milk, even some that is perfectly fine, might disgust you. This is why it's important to think about the intense emotions you experience and recognize whether or not your brain's response to a situation is accurate at the time.

"I poured some old cereal into a bowl and it had bugs all over it. I almost threw up. I was grossed out." *Steven*

At a basic level, disgust is a rejection response to something that tastes or smells bad. But this definition does not always fit. People can be disgusted by things that don't have anything to do with rotten food.

Other Triggers for Disgust

Scientists have found that humans have a disgust response to unfamiliar foods and to other issues about food, such as texture, where it comes from, and who or what may have touched it. You might love to eat sauerkraut, but your friend might think it's disgusting. A food you love that's from another country might trigger disgust in your friends just because it's unfamiliar to them. Or finding a bug on the butter might repulse you but not bother your sibling.

Other situations that can trigger disgust include smelling someone's body odor, smelling or seeing another person's bodily products (like going into the restroom and finding that someone hasn't flushed), and seeing a dead or badly injured person or animal.

Psych Notes !

Does Odor Affect Who or What You Like?

Researchers wondered if the smell of certain odors can affect how much we like particular people, places, and foods. They studied people's reactions to certain odors, and also to products that disguise body odor (like cologne and perfume). It turns out that your memory for certain odors does affect whether you like certain people, places, and foods. For example, if you love the smell of your aunt's cinnamon buns, you might really like a place or food that smells similarly. But your sense of smell may not decide if you like a person more when it comes to scented products. You may like the smell of a cologne or perfume, but it doesn't cause you to more favorably evaluate the person who wears it. So your emotional memory of a smell that's connected with something you enjoyed counts a lot. But spraying yourself with products won't necessarily make someone like you more.

Wrzesniewski, A., McCauley, C., & Rozin, P. (1999). Odor and affect: Individual differences in the impact of odor on liking for places, things, and people. *Chemical Senses, 24,* 713–721.

Moral Disgust

Certain situations where you believe someone has done something that is morally wrong (like hurting someone who is much younger and smaller) trigger moral disgust—the sense that you want to avoid the person because they are bad, hurtful, untrustworthy, or unfair. Values differ among cultures, which also influence what makes people morally disgusted. You might experience moral disgust if you play a sport or game with someone who cheats or if a friend steals something from you. When you are morally disgusted by someone's actions you are trying to protect yourself by having a response that keeps you away from that person.

Have you ever been morally disgusted with yourself? Being morally disgusted with yourself is usually linked with emotions of guilt or shame. If you betray a friend, for example, you're likely to experience guilt or shame as well as be disgusted with yourself. Since paying attention to your emotional reactions is a way to learn, think about what you can do to correct the situation or what you might do differently the next time.

Humor and Disgust

Some very humorous situations have to do with surprise—something unexpected happening—mixed with disgust. But these situations are usually only funny when you are with other people or telling someone about it later. The surprise and disgust of stepping in dog poop can be hilarious when you are with a friend, but if you are alone it is surprising and disgusting in a not-so-funny way.

Are You Easily Disgusted?

Rate your level of disgust for each of the following situations using a scale from 1 (not disgusting at all) to 5 (highly disgusting):

_____ Your little brother has head lice.

_____ Your father asks you to pick up the fish that jumped out of the aquarium.

_____ A sick kid vomits right in front of you and some of it lands on your shoes.

_____ You find someone's chewing gum stuck under your desk.

_____ Your cat brings a live rat to you.

_____ The person sitting next to you in class keeps passing gas.

_____ You walk into a restroom stall and find an unflushed toilet.

_____ Your friend does not change his socks for 5 days.

What about your score?

30–40: You're pretty easily disgusted. It's fine, so are many other people.

24–29: You're not very disgusted by most things. When you are disgusted, it's often not unbearable.

Less than 23: Not many things disgust you!

What to Do When You're Really Disgusted

When disgust threatens how you feel, it can certainly change your mood to a negative one (unless whatever disgusts you is a funny situation that you are sharing with a friend). Depending upon the situation, there are things that you can do when you are disgusted:

* *Distract yourself.* If you focus on what is disgusting you then your body is more likely to respond in a rejecting way (like gagging or throwing up). Distract yourself with conversation, music, or by thinking of something pleasant.
* *Smile.* Since disgust can be felt in your facial expression, changing your facial expression can interfere with your disgust response.
* *Be empathetic.* If your disgust is about a person, try to feel sorry for them rather than disgusted.
* *Cover your nose.* When you are disgusted by a smell, cover your nose with your hands until you become used to it. It helps to breathe out of your mouth, too.
* *Be a scientist.* If something you see is disgusting, try to create in your mind a scientific approach to it. Think "it's disgusting, but it's part of nature."

Disgust makes you want to distance yourself from whatever it is that created the strong feelings of distaste, dislike, and revulsion. As a part of being human, disgust protects you from eating anything that might be spoiled or contaminated. Moral disgust keeps you away from people who behave in ways that are offensive to you. But many humorous situations have to do with surprise mixed with disgust. So have fun with some of your emotions!

Emotions that make you feel threatened are a way for your brain to inform you to be alert and be prepared to take action. So use those strong feelings to remind yourself to be safe. Unlike threatening emotions that make you alert, the next chapters will focus on emotions that can make you feel heavy or gloomy.

In a Mood to Ponder

* What makes you anxious? What do you usually do to calm yourself down?

* Do you like to be frightened by movies or television programs? If so, do you remember them the next day when you are trying to think about something else?

* Has another person ever made you experience disgust? How might your reaction change if you felt sorry for that person?

Part four

Feeling Gloomy

left out * down * disappointed * burdened

invisible * stuck * unhappy * undeserving

depressed * heavy hearted * miserable

mournful * glum * morose * heartbroken

When you are gloomy, you might describe the feeling as heavy, as though a huge weight is on your shoulders or in your chest. You might also feel tired, like you have no energy. Some gloomy emotions are loneliness, sadness, and grief.

Loneliness, sadness, and grief are similar because of the heaviness you can feel. But there are differences mostly because of what causes you to experience those emotions. We'll talk about these causes in the next chapters.

If you are lonely, you can feel isolated and like you don't have friends who understand you. Everything around you might seem empty when you're lonely. When you're sad, everything might seem kind of dark and dreary, and you experience distress, suffering, or regret because of an event or a circumstance. Grief is an emotion that has to do with intense sadness because of a loss of someone or something important to you.

You might want to avoid feeling gloomy, hoping the feelings will disappear if you just refuse to pay attention to them. Loneliness, sadness, and grief are difficult to ignore and it's also normal to experience them. Understanding these intense emotions, and the strong feelings that come along with them, might help you find better ways to cope.

Chapter 10

Loneliness

When you are lonely you feel disconnected, left out, or distant from other people. Loneliness can make you feel like someone or something is missing. You can feel sad or empty on the inside. You really want someone to hang out with someone who will understand and like you. Sometimes though, you can be lonely even when you have friends if you just don't feel close to them.

Loneliness can feel as though it might never end. You might even begin to feel unwanted or not important since being connected to friends can make you feel good about yourself.

"I moved from another state and left my friends. I'm really lonely." *Marco*

Being Alone and Being Lonely

There are times when you may want to be alone, but wanting to spend time with yourself is quite different than the experience of loneliness. People choose to be alone, but probably no one would choose to be lonely. You may want to be alone because you want to rest, think, or

Psych Notes !

When Friendships Make You Lonely

Maybe you think that anyone with a lot of friends couldn't possibly be lonely, but that's not always the case. Researchers found that some kids look like they are surrounded by friends, but their relationships are distressing, disappointing, and make them unhappy. Being terribly stressed about social relationships can make you lonely, even though on the outside no one else would suspect it. So loneliness is not simply about having no friends. It can also involve how you feel about the relationships that you do have. If you are lonely or feel disconnected, even though you have many friends, step back and think about the ways in which you can connect with them emotionally. Or branch out to form friendships with others who may better connect with you.

Parker, J. G., & Asher, S. R. (1993). Friendship and friendship quality in middle childhood: Links with peer group acceptance and feelings of loneliness and social dissatisfaction. *Developmental Psychology, 29,* 611–621; and Davis, M. H., & Franzoi, S. L. (1986). Adolescent loneliness, self-disclosure, and private self-consciousness: A longitudinal investigation. *Journal of Personality and Social Psychology, 51,* 595–608.

do something creative by yourself. But loneliness makes you crave connection with other people. Being alone can be peaceful and quiet, and at times may even be a relief when you are feeling especially insecure around others.

Some people have a difficult time being alone or spending time with themselves. They may become anxious unless friends are around, thinking that they have to constantly be with friends so that they won't lose them and end up lonely. So anxiety that you might become isolated and lonely is different than the actual emotion of loneliness. But if you have a huge need to stay connected because you're so uncomfortable when you're not, then you might be with someone just to avoid your own anxiety about becoming lonely. In this case, it's important that you take a look at where your anxiety comes from. For example, you may believe that people are going to leave you because of a past experience that led your brain to have that expectation.

What You Can Do About Your Loneliness

Loneliness is a tough emotion. You might feel disconnected from the whole world and it might seem like there's no escaping the feeling. But there are things you can do to dig yourself out of loneliness:

* *Talk about who you are and push yourself to open up.* Having relationships keeps you from being lonely if you can share your thoughts and feelings. If you and another person are connected in this way, you are likely to experience the relationship as supportive as well as feel known.
* *Reach out.* You are more likely to connect with others if you express a friendly attitude, smile, and make eye contact. Call or text someone you know and invite them over. Even if they can't come over, at least they'll know that you are interested in a friendship.
* *Join a club or an organization and participate.* People who have a common purpose often end up as friends.
* *Connect to your family.* Being connected with family members can make you feel more secure and it may help to reduce some of the pressure while you find important friendships with peers.

Loneliness is experienced as a feeling of isolation, emptiness, and a longing for closeness with others. Although loneliness is usually thought of as having no friendships, you can feel lonely in a group of friends if you don't feel understood and emotionally connected with them.

Do You Reach Out When You're Lonely?

Check *true* or *false* in response to the following statements that describe what you might do if you're lonely:

TRUE   FALSE

_____ _____ If I am lonely, I will call someone I know.

_____ _____ If I moved somewhere and didn't know anyone, I might volunteer at a place where I could help people or animals.

_____ _____ I believe that other kids are lonely too. It could make someone happy if I tried to connect with them.

_____ _____ Rather than stay at home, I might walk around outside or go somewhere if I am lonely.

_____ _____ Even if it's hard to do, I try to introduce myself to kids or at least smile.

_____ _____ If I moved, I'd let kids know that I'm new to that place.

What about your score?

If you answered *true* to four or more of the statements, you are making a good effort to connect with other people when you are lonely.

If you answered *true* to three or less of the statements, you might be waiting for others to reach out to you. But you may have to be the one who reaches out when you are lonely.

Loneliness certainly does feel gloomy and heavy. And sometimes the feelings created by loneliness are also felt when you are sad. Sadness will be discussed in the next chapter.

Chapter 11

Sadness

Sadness is an emotion that you might have in response to loss or disappointment. You might be sad because your best friend moved away, the vacation you looked forward to all year was cancelled, or because you were rejected by someone you really liked. When something happens that really hurts or disappoints you, you will be sad simply because you really cared. It seems you're helpless to do anything about it.

Feeling Your Sadness

Sometimes sadness is described as something that makes you feel heavy hearted because when you're sad you might have a heavy feeling in your chest, as though your tears are caught up inside of you. The gloomy feelings that come with sadness make you feel tired and uninterested in stuff that usually makes you happy. You may have to try extra hard to get things done when you are sad. Some people become embarrassed if they are sad, because they think being sad means that you are weak. Sadness does make you feel somewhat helpless or powerless, but you are supposed to be sad in response to some things in life.

As an emotion, it's hard to know what purpose sadness serves. Some psychologists believe that sadness is a response to being stressed about something, and that the tired feelings that come with sadness help you to recover because you will rest or get the emotional support you need.

> "Our family planned a special trip, but we weren't able to go. I was really sad even though I tried to be understanding."
> *Heather*

Have you ever been in a situation where you have to try to cheer up? Sometimes it seems best not to show your sad feelings—like feeling down about your best friend moving away when you're around a new person who wants to be your best friend. But if you always hide your sadness, then you may not get the sympathy and support you need and deserve, even if it is just from yourself. If your family members or friends notice that you are sad and they comfort you, the connection you have with them can be relieving. Other people can make you feel better because having contact with others takes away the lonely feeling that can come with sadness.

> "I don't like feeling sad. When I am sad I like to be alone in my room." *Junior*

When You Aren't Sad in a Sad Situation

> "My friend is really sad because his girlfriend broke up with him." *Jayden*

What if you don't express sadness when you should be? Maybe you're just using other emotions, like anger, to cover it up. You might become angry or irritable if you're uncomfortable with the sadness you're feeling. And it can be really confusing to you and the people around you.

Crying Can Be Confusing

People often cry when they experience an intense emotion like sadness. However, there are many situations where crying may involve emotions other than sadness. You might be angry or frustrated, but if you believe that expressing those feelings is unacceptable at the moment, you cry instead. But then you might feel embarrassed that you cried, as well as misunderstood, since your expression of emotion does not fit with what you really feel. On the other hand, there may be a circumstance that triggers sadness and makes you feel like crying, but if crying seems unacceptable to you, instead you might express another emotion, such as anger.

Many people just can't stop themselves when they want to cry, and others seem to have a lot of willpower to control their tears. Crying expresses how you feel inside—feelings that you may not want others to see. Do you feel okay about crying when you have strong feelings?

Some boys are taught to be tough and to hide their sensitivity. Unfortunately, they may end up believing that crying expresses weakness. Or they may try to appear as though they can't be hurt emotionally. Remember talking about how emotions are expressed differently depending on a person's culture? The same goes for crying. In some cultures, crying is acceptable for girls, but many boys hold back their tears.

> "I was really sad when my mom and dad got divorced. But I didn't want to cry because I didn't want to seem like a wimp. Then I got mean to my friends. They made excuses to not hang out with me and couldn't tell me why. I just held in my feelings and was grumpy and angry."
> *Lillian*

Would You Put a Guy Down If He Cried?

You may believe that crying is as acceptable for boys as it is for girls. But even though you may know that something is logically correct—that of course it is okay for anyone to cry—your attitude may be different in certain situations. Answer the following statements *true* or *false*, then total your answers:

TRUE   **FALSE**

_____   _____   It is healthy for a guy to hold back his tears if a girl breaks up with him.

_____   _____   Watching my mom cry is easier than it is to see my dad cry.

_____   _____   When guys cry, they lose a little bit of my respect.

_____   _____   Most boys only want to cry when they are angry, frustrated, or physically hurt.

_____   _____   I'd give a hug to a tearful girl but I probably wouldn't hug a guy who is crying.

_____   _____   When I was in elementary school, if a boy cried a lot I might secretly think that he was a "cry-baby."

_____   _____   TOTAL

What about your score?

If you answered three or more of the questions as *true*, you may think that boys should not show their vulnerability with tears. If so, why do you think you have that view?

Sadness and Depression

Sadness and depression are not the same, although people often use either word to describe their gloomy feelings of sadness. In contrast to sadness, which happens in response to a certain situation or event, depression is more like a long-lasting mood that can occur without anything happening that clearly triggers it. Depression can feel like a very long-lasting sadness. If your sadness gets in the way of finding pleasure in your life or feels too strong and out of control, talk to your parents. They could arrange for you to talk to a professional therapist or counselor who can help you through this tough time.

Moving on From Feeling Sad

If you are sad about something and want to move on from your sadness, here are a few things you can do:

* *Think about your sadness.* Take a moment to acknowledge your sadness and why you are sad. Imagine that your brain is trying to get you to pay attention to what you are feeling, so you can accept it and let it go.
* *Focus your attention on activities.* Whether it is cleaning your room, playing soccer, or doing homework, do something to keep busy. If your mind starts to drift to your sad feelings, just get yourself back on track and remind yourself that later you will give yourself time to think about your sad feelings.
* *Connect with others.* Talk about how you feel with a parent or a good friend. Getting together with a friend or hanging out with your family can help relieve sadness.

Can You Feel Sad and Happy at the Same Time?

Researchers studied whether emotions really can occur at the same time. They found that there are lots of situations when a person can feel two emotions at once. So imagine that you are graduating from elementary school and going on to middle school. You may be sad if you are leaving teachers or friends, but happy and excited that you are going to a new school. While it might feel strange, you can experience two emotions at the same time!

Larsen, J. T., McGraw, A. P., & Cacioppo, J. T. (2001). Can people feel happy and sad at the same time? *Journal of Personality and Social Psychology, 81,* 684–696.

When you experience an event that involves a loss or disappointment, you are likely to be sad. Sharing your feelings with others when you are sad takes away the sense of being alone. Intense sadness is experienced with grief, another emotion that makes you feel gloomy.

Chapter 12

Grief

Grief is an emotion of very intense sadness that you experience in response to the loss of someone you love or something that is highly treasured. If someone you love dies, you may have a very difficult time making sense of the situation. You may expect to see that person in places they've been before. You might even think of getting together with them, and then realize that it's not possible. If you lose someone you love, your longing to have that person back might even make you imagine that something, such as a certain noise, means that the person is still here. But strong feelings of sadness may remind you that your loss is in fact real. Such reactions to grief are normal and understandable as a person tries to adjust to a big loss.

"My grandfather died 2 weeks ago and I just can't get over it. I think about him all the time and I can't concentrate on anything else."
Juan

Feeling Your Grief

Grief makes you feel heavy, empty, and tired. You are likely to be very sad even when something good is happening around you. When you are grieving you might find it very hard to focus or concentrate on things. You can even feel as though you aren't interested in your favorite foods or activities. At other times you might be angry or irritable, even though you hardly ever used to feel that way.

When grief is intense you might just feel numb when you expect to have strong feelings of sadness. Feeling nothing when you should be feeling a lot can be confusing. Some people then become guilty if their feelings are numb when something bad has happened. But feeling numb in situations like this is normal, and other feelings return when you are not so overwhelmed by your loss.

Adapting to Loss

Mourning is the time where you gradually adapt to a loss. This process usually includes thinking through and facing the reality of the loss, expressing emotions, and becoming active in life again. However, it's also normal for grieving to last a lifetime as a kind of sadness in the back of your mind that does not get in the way of how you function in your daily life. So it may not be accurate to think that you ever just "get over" a loss, because you can't erase your emotional memories. For example, if you visit a place that reminds you of the person you miss in your life, your grief may become triggered. Certain dates can remind you of your loss, such as the person's birthday or the date the person died. You can find ways to sooth memories of a loss, you can distract yourself, or you can create new memories. But you're not going to totally get over it because that's impossible. Besides, it's not about getting over a loss. Instead, you have to adapt, continue moving forward in your life, and accept your sadness when memories of your loss are triggered.

What Would You Do About Your Grief?

Imagine you have lost someone who is special in your life. Check *true* or *false* to the following statements about some of the things you might do:

TRUE   FALSE

_____ _____ I'd have a notebook where I could write my memories of times with that person.

_____ _____ I'd think about a great quality that person had, and I'd try to be that way myself.

_____ _____ I would have a special box where I'd put things that reminded me of that person.

_____ _____ I'd do something special to remember the person I lost on his or her birthday.

_____ _____ I would say a prayer for the person I lost.

_____ _____ If I felt like crying, I wouldn't hold it back.

_____ _____ I would talk about the person to others who knew him or her, and sometimes to people who didn't know the person I lost.

_____ _____ I might smile about something really good or fun about them that I remember whenever I think about them.

_____ _____ I would not push away my thoughts about the person I lost.

What about your score?

If you answered five or more of the statements as *true*, you have some tools to use that would help you to cope with a loss.

If you answered five or more of the statements *false* or if you would like to have more tools you can use to cope with loss, read the next section about what to do when you lose someone you love.

What to Do When You Lose Someone You Love

When you lose someone you love, you want most to go back in time and have that person in your life again. Knowing it is impossible makes you very aware of being helpless. There are some things you can do to help you get through this tough time (and those times in the future when you are reminded of your loss). Most of these things have to do with remembering the person you lost, instead of trying to forget about your loss or push aside your memories:

* Remember what you learned from the person you lost.
* Do some of the things you enjoyed doing with that person, and try to copy some of the things he or she enjoyed doing.
* Make a box or folder that includes reminders about the person. Draw a picture, write a story, or make some notes about special memories.
* Create a special place in your room where you can put things that remind you of the person you lost.
* Cry if you feel like crying. Crying lets other people know that you need their comforting.
* Talk with an adult you trust, and share that you are having a hard time with grief. Sometimes just talking about what you are going through can help you to sort out your emotions.
* Don't be surprised or worried if a feeling related to your grief comes up again even years later. Certain places, times of the year, or holidays may trigger an emotional reaction that reminds you of your loss.

Pet Loss Can Be Intense

The experience of grief caused by the death of a pet can be just as intense as the loss of a human in a kid's life, according to researchers. Young people can form very strong bonds with their pets. Pets provide affection and consistency. They are always there for you, including when you are having a tough time dealing with something. You probably could have guessed the researchers' conclusion that the more bonded you are with your pet, the more intense your experience of loss will be if it dies. But they also stress the importance of sharing the feelings you have in response to the loss of a pet, which many people tend to ignore compared to their human losses. If your pet dies, let your family and friends know that you need their support.

Brown, B. H., Richards, H. C., & Wilson, C. A. (1996). Pet bonding and pet bereavement among adolescents. *Journal of Counseling & Development, 74,* 505–510.

When Your Pet Dies

When a pet dies, your feelings can be just as strong as when you lose a member of your family because pets are like family members. People might try to make you feel better (but it doesn't help) by telling you that you can get another pet. Although you will love another pet, you probably realize that the one you lost had a unique personality and can never be replaced.

"My cat died and I have been sad for a month."
Adina

Loneliness, sadness, and grief make you feel heavy, tired, and gloomy. Loneliness makes you feel empty, sadness can make you feel helpless, and grief can make you feel intensely sad. Hopefully you will use some of the tips in the last few chapters if or when you have the strong feelings that come with these emotions. Finding your happy, positive feelings again is important when life is tough. The next chapters on elated feelings are about some positive emotions.

In a Mood to Ponder

* What advice would you give to someone who goes to a new school and doesn't know anyone? Would you reach out to a new kid in your class?

* When you are sad do you let anyone know how you feel? Do you find yourself avoiding the things you usually like to do?

* Have you ever lost someone or something in your life who meant a lot to you—like a person or pet? What are some things you learned from that relationship?

Part five

Feeling Elated!

giddy * thrilled * delighted * optimistic
crazed * cheerful * joyful * enthused
positive * energized * blissful * smitten
energized * ecstatic * hyper * hopeful

Some of your emotions are especially positive. Elated emotions, such as excitement, joy, happiness, infatuation, and love can make you feel light, energetic, and optimistic. In various ways, these emotions are triggered by experiences that give you intense pleasure, connect you in a positive way with other people, or give meaning to your life.

Focusing on what kinds of experiences bring out strong positive emotions in you is important in your life. Positive emotions can elevate your mood or can help a bad mood to disappear. So they can strongly influence how you interact with everyone around you, and they can make you become more social or friendly just because of how you feel. The good feelings you have from positive emotions can motivate you, make it easier to get things done, and can help you through tough times.

Chapter 13

Excitement, Joy, and Happiness

You've just found out that you won a contest or that your best friend won't be moving away after all. Excitement, joy, and happiness are often triggered by experiences that give you intense pleasure, connect you in a positive way with other people, or give meaning to your life—something that gives you a purpose or a goal. So you might experience one of these emotions in response to an accomplishment, a call from a new friend, being with people you really like, getting something that you had wished for, helping others, or just laughing with friends or family members.

Feeling Joyful, Excited, and Happy

When you experience joy, excitement, or happiness, you are likely to feel energetic and become optimistic, positive, and hopeful about what lies ahead. You may smile, laugh, and feel light hearted.

Psych Notes !

Smiling Can Make You Happier

You know that your emotions create certain facial expressions, such as smiling when you are happy. But it is also true that facial expressions can cause you to experience an emotion. Researchers have found that if you make a facial expression that closely resembles the pattern of muscles that are used to express a particular emotion, then there's a good chance you might feel that emotion. So if you want to feel happier, especially when you are down, put a smile on your face.

Ekman, P. (1993). Facial expression and emotion. *American Psychologist, 48,* 384–392.

Creating Happiness With Optimism

You don't have to wait around for an event, a good grade, a wish that comes true, or even for someone else's attention in order to be happier. It takes practice, but you can learn to be more positive, optimistic, and happy. Finding ways to feel good and keep your spirit up when you are stressed out is also important.

Think Happy Thoughts

Part of feeling happy has a lot to do with how you think. Finding the positive side of a situation can help you feel better about it. For example, two people can experience the same situation, and one of them will try to find something positive about it, and the other may focus on everything that's negative. Guess who is likely to feel better about it?

What Makes You Happy?

Mark the following statements *true* or *false*:

TRUE	FALSE	
_____	_____	If I could live this year over again, I would change a lot of things.
_____	_____	If I had more of something (like clothes or computers), I'd be happier.
_____	_____	Wealthy people are probably happier.
_____	_____	If I could spend more time with friends, I'd be happy.
_____	_____	I would be happy if my family lived in a different town.
_____	_____	I think I'd be happier if I looked different.
_____	_____	When the weather is cold and rainy, I am not happy.

What about your score?

If five or more of your answers are *false*, you probably find happiness with what you have in life and don't wait for something to come along or change in order for you to be happy.

If five or more of your answers are *true*, then you may be waiting for something outside of yourself to make you happy. Spend some time thinking about what you can do right now to make yourself happier.

Adjusting your attitude toward thinking in a more optimistic way is a habit you can develop. When you feel defeated, disappointed, or frustrated think about what you learned from the situation. Give yourself credit for trying and for doing your best. For most experiences, there will probably be a next time when you can try again. So when things don't go your way, think about what you learned, what you might do differently next time, and how you can improve.

When Happiness Turns Negative

You may want to be optimistic about a situation and imagine that it will have a happy ending. However, there are times when a situation may remind you of something similar in the past where the outcome

Psych Notes !

Do You Want to Be Happier?

Focus on little things each day that give you a moment of positive feeling like hanging out in the warmth of the sun, laughing with a friend, or watching a funny movie. Researchers found that people who focused on moments of good feeling were better able to handle challenges and manage their stress. You don't have to deny that negative things happen, but simply remembering to notice the moments when something makes you excited, joyful, happy, or even just appreciative will likely improve your overall mood and will help you to deal with setbacks.

Cohn, M. A., Fredrickson, B. L., Brown, S. L., Mikels, J. A., & Conway, A. M. (2009). Happiness unpacked: Positive emotions increase life satisfaction by building resilience. *Emotion, 9,* 361–368.

was negative. For example, let's say that for 2 weekends in a row, your favorite cousin was planning to visit, but both times your aunt had to work and couldn't bring him. He is planning to come next weekend, but you aren't excited this time. Your appraisal system may expect that the same thing is going to happen again, so instead of being excited, you are already planning to be disappointed. This is one of those times when you have to realize that your brain is evaluating the situation and just trying to alert you to the possibility of another disappointment. But it does not mean that you will be disappointed. So try to find your happy and excited feelings again.

It can seem like such a waste to get nervous about good things, but it happens all of the time. If you are really excited about something, you might become afraid that you will do something to make it go away or that you don't deserve it in the first place. So as a result you become anxious instead. For example, if you are really excited about going to a dance with the person you like, you might worry that you are going to do something that will embarrass yourself.

Now, it's normal to get anxious when you're excited or joyful about something. But don't let worry take over your happiness. Learn how to enjoy a great feeling without taking it away from yourself with negative thoughts. Negative or worried thoughts spoil a good mood.

If you find your happiness turning negative, here's what you can do:

* Remind yourself to enjoy the good feeling. Remember that you deserve to feel happy and excited! Keep reminding yourself of this to push the negative thoughts away.

> "I have a school dance coming up. I asked this boy to the dance. He said yes! I was so happy. But when I got off the phone with him I got nervous that I might trip or fall over in front of him or something."
> *Esmeralda*

* Pay attention to what concerns you and consider what you will do about it.
* Think about the worst thing that might happen. Usually, you will find that the possibility of a bad thing happening is really very small.
* If you continue to worry, make a plan for what you might do if something goes wrong.

The emotions of excitement and joy, or a happy mood, can be triggered when you have pleasurable and meaningful experiences in your life. Can being in love or infatuated with someone make you happy? You already know the answer to that question! But you may not know some things about love and infatuation that will be discussed in the next chapter.

Love and Infatuation

Chapter 14

Defining what love is can be very difficult because the word is used in many different ways. You may use the word "love" in describing how you feel about your family, a friend, the person you really like, your parakeet, or chocolate cake. So coming up with a precise definition may depend upon why you are using the word. Scientists are still trying to figure out if love is one emotion, a mixture of emotions, an attitude, a learned behavior, or something that comes from an *innate ability*—something we are born with—that emotionally attaches us to other people.

By the time you are a preteen, you'll have probably experienced an infatuation—being powerfully interested in, fascinated by, or kind of obsessed with another person. Infatuations (crushes or really liking someone) are related to the feelings people have when they describe certain kinds of love—those where you think about the other person a lot of the time and want the other person to feel the same way about you. But what's the difference between love and an infatuation?

Feeling Love and Infatuations

When people feel as though they are "in love," they may have a strong attraction to another person, and also may care very much about him or her. Most often, being in love involves having fond or tender feelings as well as compassion toward someone you know well (how you love your grandma or best friend). Loving behaviors can involve caring, attraction, and warm feelings that attach us to others.

As opposed to love, infatuations are based on being attracted to another person in superficial ways, such how the person looks. The feelings you have are usually temporary, even though at the time you may think that the feeling will last forever. When people have an infatuation they may say that they are "in love," but they're just using a figure of speech. People usually think of love as much more involved than an infatuation.

Infatuations are exciting. They elevate your mood and can make you happy and positive like you're walking on air and nothing can make you feel bad. When you see the person you like, you might feel butterflies in your stomach because infatuations can make you anxious and excited. There is often a lot of time spent looking forward to something happening when you are infatuated, such as seeing or talking to that other person, and figuring out if the other person feels that same way about you.

Both infatuations and feelings of love are not always reasonable. An infatuation allows your imagination to make someone seem just perfect. If you don't know someone very well and have not spent a lot of time with that person, then you can imagine they are whoever you want them to be. You might possibly experience a loving feeling toward another person that is created by your imagination, and it can be just as strong as the love you feel toward someone you know very well. This can make feelings of love very confusing.

Psych Notes !

What Attracts You to Certain People?

Researchers have found that deep in your brain are memories that may explain why you may have loving feelings for, or infatuations with, certain people and not others. These memories are called "implicit memories," which means that they are memories outside of your awareness, even though they still can affect your choices. For example, if your favorite dinner is macaroni and cheese—the way your dad makes it—when you grow up, you may have a special craving for that particular kind of mac-and-cheese.

The implicit memories that are formed by relationships are similar. Your loving feelings toward your caregivers may be connected with their specific mannerisms and personality traits that become buried memories in your brain. Suppose your grandfather took care of you early in your life and he would sing to you in a certain way that made you feel really loved. Much later in your life, you may become attracted to people who like to sing. These qualities that attract you to other people are made up of memories that are imprinted on the limbic system of your brain—the center of your emotions. So it is no wonder that scientists tell us that love and infatuation are very complicated!

Lewis, T., Amini, F., & Lannon, R. (2000). *A general theory of love*. New York, NY: Random House.

Are You Infatuated?

Think about the person who you're really into while answering the following questions *true* or *false*:

TRUE   FALSE

_____ _____ I don't really know the person I really like, but I like the way that person looks or the way they act around others (like they are nice).

_____ _____ I look forward to possibly seeing the person I like and think about that every day.

_____ _____ I get very nervous or jittery whenever I am around the person.

_____ _____ The person I like seems just perfect.

_____ _____ Whenever my mind wanders, I think about the person I like.

What about your score?

If you answered *true* to three or more of the questions, look out! You are probably infatuated. It doesn't take much to be infatuated with someone, just a lot of imagination and focus. Don't forget that all that imagination and focus belongs to you! Do you use those good qualities for any other purpose?

Infatuation and Obsession

Whether it's love or an infatuation, there are situations where you may find you can't get the other person out of your mind. When a person can't get something out of their mind, and they think about it constantly, psychologists call those thoughts "obsessive." Most people occasionally obsess about something because it is their mind's way of figuring out a problem or dealing with all the feelings that a situation creates. Obsessing about a person with whom you are infatuated can feel good if you are thinking about the exciting part, or it can be upsetting if you are thinking about things that didn't go the way you had wished.

If you become obsessed with an infatuation you have with someone it can direct your thoughts in unusual ways. You may become preoccupied with thoughts about the person you like and have trouble concentrating on the things you have to do because you'd much rather be thinking about them. Friends can get sick of your stories about your infatuation and your concern about wanting that person to notice you.

If you find yourself obsessing about someone so much that you are not paying attention to important things, then you might want to find a way to become more balanced. Here is what you can do if you become obsessed with your infatuation:

* Create a schedule. With a schedule, you can assign yourself a certain time when you'll think only about that person, another time period to think about your homework, and time when your mind can be occupied with other activities. Seriously focus on the other things that you need to think about, and keep reminding yourself that you will have time to think about that person later.

"Today in dance class I got to dance with a guy I like. I was so happy that I didn't want to wash my hands."
Tamara

"The guy I like handed me a present for my birthday. Afterward I felt like I was walking on air."
Valerie

* Remember to think about yourself. What do you admire about yourself? What will another person admire about you? Consider ways in which you can improve to admire yourself more.

* Make sure you are not getting caught up in an infatuation in order to avoid something that may need your attention. Sometimes being obsessed with someone else is a way to avoid things that you don't want to think about.

Generally, love is experienced as a deep caring about someone or something. Infatuations often feel like love, but usually those feelings are the result of who you imagine the other person to be.

The next section is about emotions that are not so positive— the stormy emotions of anger, jealousy, and envy.

In a Mood to Ponder

* What makes you happy? Does your happiness usually depend upon the actions of other people? In what ways do you create happiness for yourself?

* The next time you are in a situation where you laugh hard, notice your good mood. How can you have more laughter in your life?

* Would you describe yourself as an optimistic person— someone who thinks positive and hopeful thoughts about the future? Why or why not?

* Have you ever been infatuated with someone? What qualities does that person have that you like? Did you ever wish that you had those qualities yourself?

Part six

Feeling Stormy

annoyed * irritated * upset * hurt

impatient * frustrated * aggravated

bothered * unloved * discouraged

neglected * rejected * put down

bitter * resentful

The emotions of anger, jealousy, and envy are intense and stormy. The strong feelings they create seem to take control of your body and your thoughts. In a very negative way, you might become preoccupied with how you feel and think about someone or something. These emotions are usually experienced in situations that have to do with other people, and when you are especially vulnerable.

Stormy emotions can make you feel out of control of what you say or do. In fact, you might say or do something when you feel these intense emotions that later you'll regret. That's why it's important to keep your head when you are angry, jealous, or envious. As you read this chapter on these stormy emotions, remember that your emotions give you information that helps you to protect yourself. So if you feel an intense, stormy emotion, something is happening that puts you on alert. Understanding yourself at those times will help you use your strong feelings in a way that doesn't lead to you being misunderstood, looking bad, or hurting someone.

Chapter 15

Anger

Anger can make you feel as though you are burning up inside or as though you are very powerful. Your body might tense up and you might even get a stomachache. Anger can stay with you for a long time or it can hide under the surface and get triggered when you are reminded of the thing that made you angry in the first place. The emotion of anger can feel so strong that you may have difficulty getting negative thoughts out of your mind. When you're angry, you may want to be alone or you may want to go to sleep just to get away from your own thoughts. But anger can keep you awake when you'd like to sleep, too.

You might become angry in response to frustration, threat, or competition. When something doesn't turn out the way in which you had hoped, and you just can't accept the outcome, your anger expresses that you want the situation to change. Sometimes anger covers up another emotion. You may actually be experiencing shame, sadness, guilt, fear, or jealousy, but instead you express anger.

> "I get mad a lot. It scares me, my mom, and my dog because I end up screaming. I get very loud about anything, like what clothes to wear. " *Tabitha*

> "Sometimes my dad doesn't really listen to me. He thinks he's always right. Even when I prove that I'm right, he just tells me to be quiet." *Lindsay*

What Makes You Angry?

A lot of things can make you angry—situations, people, or a bad grade. Sometimes peers can say or do things that trigger your anger. You can become angry if someone teases you, takes your things, invades your privacy, or if someone convinces you to do something you don't want to do. Many people become angry when they are hurt, shamed, rejected, stressed, or misunderstood. (Anger often follows other emotions.)

At times you might feel frustrated with your parents or other adults, especially if things don't go your way and you are powerless to change anything. You might become angry if it seems as though your feelings are not taken into consideration, or if the adults in your life just don't seem to listen or understand. Sometimes an angry mood can make you frustrated or annoyed about something, so you might lash out at your parents or siblings. People tend to show more anger around family members. You might feel safer to express negative feelings around them because you know that family members are going to be there regardless of how you behave or what you do.

Angry Behavior

People have all kinds of interesting behaviors when they are angry. Some have a habit of venting their anger and expressing it in an aggressive way as though they have to get it all out.

Some kids hold it in, often because they are thinking about the consequences if they express their anger. But sometimes anger can be very hard to hold in, and it can just blurt out in a way that you had hoped it wouldn't. In this sense, anger can lead to guilt or shame. Some people become verbally or physically out of control when they become angry, and they may take their feelings out on someone or something. They may even take it out on themselves.

Obviously, it's just as harmful to take your anger out on yourself as it is to take it out on someone else. You don't deserve to have anyone, even yourself, take anger out on you. But holding back your anger might be just as hard on you because your anger may feel stuck inside, like a big lump in your throat, chest, or stomach. You don't have to blurt out every bit of your anger, you don't have to hurt yourself or someone else, and you don't have to put up a wall to keep it inside. But it is important to learn how to express your anger in words so that others can listen to what you are feeling.

So is it better to express your anger—like kicking a wall, ripping up papers, or hitting a pillow (as some kids have told me)—or should you try to control it and keep it to yourself? Scientists have studied what happens in a person's emotional brain when they are angry. They discovered that just letting your anger burst out might feel good for the moment, but over time it stirs up your emotional brain and doesn't calm it down. So, in the short run, angry outbursts may feel good, but in the long run, they don't help you get over the feelings and move on. But keeping your anger completely to yourself may not be such a good idea either, because you are not communicating what you feel and you may end up resentful. Instead, let's find ways for you to stay in control, but still express yourself.

Does Your Anger Cut You Off?

Anger pushes others away. It might separate you from people a little too much or too often. Check whether you are *likely* or *unlikely* to respond in the ways described in the following situations:

LIKELY **UNLIKELY**

_____ _____ I get grumpy, even angry, when I lose a game that I'm playing with a friend or sibling.

_____ _____ I might stop talking to friends who don't take my side.

_____ _____ Holding in my anger can make me seem very quiet or unresponsive.

_____ _____ When I'm angry, I'd much rather watch a movie alone than with family members.

_____ _____ My family and friends avoid me when I'm angry.

_____ _____ A grade on a test that makes me angry makes it difficult to concentrate in class.

_____ _____ When someone makes me angry, it can ruin my whole day.

What about your score?

If you answered *likely* to four or more of the situations, you might be cutting yourself off from other people a bit too much with your anger. Think about ways in which you can look at situations differently, such as not taking them so personally. Consider ways in which you can express your negativity that does not end up always isolating you from others.

If you answered *unlikely* to five or more situations, your anger may not be creating a big barrier between yourself and others.

Strategies For Dealing With Anger

Some of the strategies for dealing with anger are to

* Step away from your anger and distract yourself for a while so that you do not make decisions that are simply based on that emotion. Many people find that taking deep breaths or exercising is very relieving. Stepping back from your anger and finding a way to calm down will help you to figure out what triggered that emotion in you and how to communicate what you feel. For example, ask yourself if you are angry because you are afraid, helpless, frustrated, shamed, stressed, disappointed, or hurt.
* Use "I" statements to describe what you are feeling, rather than blame or point out the faults of someone or something else. Start by saying what you ("I") feel or think. So if someone pushes you in the lunch line, instead of saying, "You're a jerk," you might instead say, "I don't like being pushed."
* Figure out a safe way to express your anger or work it out in a way that doesn't hurt anyone or anything. Remember that it is possible to express yourself without lashing out at anyone, including yourself.
* Always try to speak in a voice that is not too loud or sarcastic. An angry tone of voice makes it impossible for the other person to hear what you are saying because they will only hear the anger and not your words.
* Talk with someone about your angry feelings—a parent, friend, teacher, counselor, or even a pet.
* Stand-up for yourself. Knowing that anger is a self-protective response, next time someone teases you, realize that you are angry because you were put down and hurt, take a deep breath, and try to stay calm. Even if you very simply say that you don't appreciate being teased, then at least the focus would be on the person who made the comment, rather than on your angry response.

Anger is often a response to frustration or threat, or it can be a response to another emotion that makes you feel vulnerable. Having too much control over your anger might keep you from communicating with others and might lead you to become resentful instead. But having little control over your anger will likely cause others to misunderstand you and will push everyone away.

Like anger, envy and jealousy are emotions that are triggered when you are especially vulnerable, in competition, or have a need to protect yourself. Many people think of envy and jealousy as the same emotion, but there are important differences which will be discussed in the next chapter.

Psych Notes !

Does Getting Back At the Person Who Made You Angry Help?

When your sibling takes your things or if your best friend rejects you, you may want them to feel exactly the way they've made you feel. Anger can lead you to think about or seek revenge—to get back at the person who did or said something that caused your angry response. But will revenge really help you to feel better and move on? Psychologists have found that thinking about punishing someone, or even punishing them, will cause you to continue focusing on your anger towards that person. So wanting revenge or seeking it will keep you from moving on. The researchers also discovered that people who do not wish to punish others think less about those who angered them, and so they are able to move on. The next time you want to get back at someone, realize that you are only hurting yourself. When you stop thinking about the person who made you so angry and begin focusing on other things, you're also making them less important.

Carlsmith, K. M., Wilson, T. D., & Gilbert, D. T. (2008). The paradoxical consequences of revenge. *Journal of Personality and Social Psychology, 95,* 1316–1324.

Chapter 16

Envy and Jealousy

Envy and jealousy can make you feel stormy inside and preoccupied with negative thoughts. When you are envious or jealous you might feel threatened, insecure, rejected, inferior, out of control, and just not yourself. Both of these emotions involve your relationships with others, but they are different in important ways.

Feeling Envy

Envy has to do with feeling unhappy about the success of someone else or about what they have and, at the same time, secretly feeling inferior yourself. Instead of finding success for yourself or improving yourself, you may be envious and want what another person has, or find yourself wishing that the other person would lose what he or she has in order to make things seem fair.

If you are envious of someone you may want to put that person down as though this will raise you up or lower everyone else's opinion of them. But it just doesn't work! Instead you may want to consider that you are envious and not feeling so great about yourself (like feeling inferior or not good enough). When you envy another person you are comparing yourself to them. We really can't know what another person's life is like, but an envious person just assumes that the other person is happier or better. So in a strange way, when you envy someone else you are giving them a compliment. But it's a compliment that can harm you and how you feel about yourself.

Feeling Jealousy

Unlike envy, which has to do with wanting another person's qualities, success, or possession, jealousy has to do with thinking you will lose, or have lost, some affection or security from one person because of someone else. If you have something that other people might want, such as a friendship or someone you really like, you may feel jealous if you think other people could take it away by becoming more important to that person than you are. So often the emotions of jealousy and anxiety occur together.

When it comes to friendships, some people can become jealous and think that they must have the total attention and loyalty of a friend, otherwise the friend might become attached to someone else and go away. But if you hold on too tight to another person, she may feel trapped, instead of feeling secure, and this can cause her to want a different relationship. Jealousy, and the possessiveness that comes with it, can actually create the very thing that you may dread the most. It can push people away.

Are You Likely to Be Envious?

Check *true* or *false* in answer to the following questions:

TRUE	FALSE	
_____	_____	Situations are often unfair to me.
_____	_____	Many times I find myself wishing for what someone else has.
_____	_____	I believe that I lack important qualities that I see in others.
_____	_____	I put down others a lot, especially if I secretly admire them.
_____	_____	Others seem to get what they need when I don't.
_____	_____	Often I feel as though I am "less than" another person.
_____	_____	TOTAL

What about your score?

If you answered four or more of the questions as *true*, you may be feeling envious, which is likely to get in the way of your relationships with others as well as interfere with the relationship you have with yourself. Consider what you are noticing about others that you may admire. How can you develop those qualities in yourself? Think about ways you can improve to become a better version of yourself.

Are You Likely to Be Jealous?

Check *true* or *false* in answer to the following questions:

TRUE   **FALSE**

_____   _____   I wonder if my best friend is loyal to me.

_____   _____   When I like someone I feel insecure if I see that person paying attention to somebody else.

_____   _____   I think I am more uncertain about myself than other kids are.

_____   _____   I put down others when I am with a close friend or with someone I like.

_____   _____   It seems that others keep their close relationships and I can't.

_____   _____   When a friend doesn't call me back, I worry that he or she doesn't like me anymore.

_____   _____   TOTAL

What about your score?
If you answered four or more of the questions as *true*, you may be experiencing jealousy in your relationships. Is the insecurity you feel because of the kind of people you choose (they aren't really loyal), or does your insecurity push them away? Focus on your own good qualities and what you want in a relationship.

Feeling Envy and Jealousy Together

Sometimes envy and jealousy can be experienced in the same situation. For example, a friend may be jealous of the relationship you have with someone you like. But in such situations, your friend might tease you because they are hurt that you pay less attention to them because you have a new focus. So they may be jealous of the person you like, and envious of your new relationship. (And by the way, if you start a new relationship try to consider the feelings of your old friends, especially if you want to keep them.)

Self-doubt, loneliness, sadness, or anger can come along with envy or jealousy because you may feel as though you are lacking something in yourself or missing someone's attention. Yes, it's natural for people to hide such feelings from themselves and to feel bitter or resentful toward others instead. But it's dangerous and can become overpowering. It can push people away, making you downright unhappy and a little lonely.

"Every time I talk about my other good friends, my friend says, 'I'm your only best friend.' One time another friend of mine wrote her name with the words 'best friend' on my binder and she got mad and told me to cross it out."
Nadia

Envy, Jealousy, and Competition

When kids compete, they want to win or be the best. Many people are at their best when they are most competitive. Everyone competes differently. Some kids are motivated to be the best at nearly everything they do and really stress out about it. Sometimes a kid's need to be on top can even get in the way of being happy for someone else when he or she succeeds, best friend included! Then there are those who shy away from competition and might even be afraid to compete. You don't necessarily have to compete with others but you can compete with yourself by trying to perform your best.

What happens when a person wants to be the best but believes that there is not enough room for everyone to be successful or happy? They may look or act very mean when actually they are just afraid that they will not get what they want or need for themselves, or that they will lose what they have. In other words, they get envious and jealous of the people who they think are more successful than they are.

Situations where people are in competition can bring out parts of their personality that they do not normally express. You may find yourself losing control of who you are when you are in a competitive situation. If so, you need to step back, take a look at what you want, and decide if your behavior helps you reach that goal or defeats you. You may also have to realistically think about whether or not your goal is worth who you become in this situation. Knowing you're doing your best and focusing on yourself and not others can help keep envy and jealousy away.

Psych Notes !

Envy Can Turn You "Green"

You've probably noticed that some kids follow the lead of popular kids in what they do, how they act, or even in the clothes or products they buy. If someone has the social status you envy and you notice that they buy "green" products—ones that benefit the planet, like a reusable lunch bag or a binder covered in fabric made of recycled material—would you be more likely to go green? Researchers found that in order to gain envied social status, the people they studied were more likely purchase environmentally friendly products when they were shopping in public. So if being green becomes a status symbol, people who envy others who are green might be more environmentally conscious about what they buy.

Griskevicius, V., Tybur, J. M., & Van den Bergh B. (2010). Going green to be seen: Status, reputation, and conspicuous conservation. *Journal of Personality and Social Psychology, 98*, 392–404.

What to Do When You Are Envious or Jealous

There are a few things you might want to think about when you experience envy or jealousy:

* What does the other person have that you want for yourself? How can you get something similar for yourself without being resentful toward him or her?
* Consider how you can improve yourself to gain attention, status, or admiration from others.
* Focus on all your positive qualities. Realize that you don't have to compete with anyone else but yourself.
* What's triggering your envy or jealousy? Your brain may be responding, but that response may be based more on a past situation than on the present.

When you are envious or jealous you might feel threatened or insecure. Both envy and jealousy involve comparisons with others. You might envy a person who has something you want, or be jealous if you fear that you will be replaced by someone else in a relationship that you have with another person.

In a Mood to Ponder

* When you are angry, do you tend to hold in your feelings or let them out?

* What qualities in your personality might make someone envious?

* Have you ever had a situation where you thought that someone was jealous of you?

Conclusion

Keep Learning About Yourself

Did you even imagine how complex emotions could be? I hope the knowledge you've gained about your intense emotions and strong feelings will improve how you make decisions, help you to take action, and make it easier for you to achieve your goals.

I'm also hopeful that you're better able to understand the emotions of other people and manage your relationships. If a sibling, friend, or parent (or even you!) expresses an intense emotion, you may be able to figure out why the emotion was triggered and whether or not it seemed correct for the situation. It's likely you'll notice if their feelings were expressed with a level of intensity that helped them to be understood. Rather than get totally confused or frustrated when someone misinterprets a situation and responds with an intense emotion that just doesn't seem right, you can now understand what happened and talk it out. And you can identify when you might have had an emotional misfire, too.

Intense emotions and the strong feelings they create are complicated and fascinating. The more you learn about your emotions, the better you will understand yourself and discover how amazing you are!